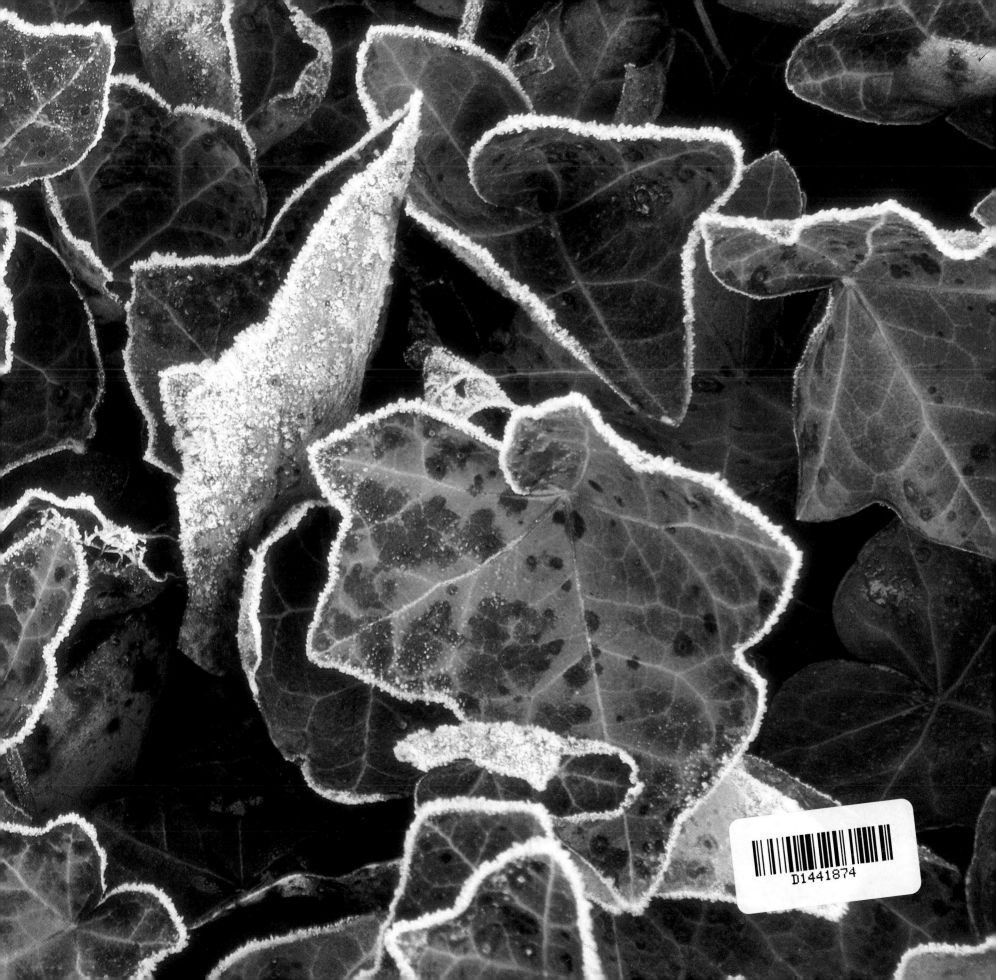

PATTERNS
IN
NATURE

PATTERNS IN NATURE

Marcus Schneck

CRESCENT BOOKS

NEW YORK

*This 1991 edition published by CRESCENT BOOKS
distributed by Outlet Book Company, Inc.,
a Random House Company,
225 Park Avenue South, New York, New York 10003*

*ISBN 0-517-06572-X
8 7 6 5 4 3 2 1*

Printed and bound in Hong Kong

*For rights information about the photographs in
this book please contact:*

*The Image Bank
111 Fifth Avenue, New York, NY 10003*

Producer: *Solomon M. Skolnick*
Writer: *Marcus Schneck*
Designer: *Ann-Louise Lipman*
Editor: *Joan E. Ratajack*
Production: *Valerie Zars*
Photo Researcher: *Edward Douglas*
Assistant Photo Researcher: *Robert V. Hale*
Editorial Assistant: *Carol Raguso*

i. *Gigantic bracken fern, Purakarenui Falls Park,
South Island, New Zealand* ii. *Cottony clouds as
they reflect the colors of a setting sun*

TABLE OF CONTENTS

An accurate variation of that old cliché "nature abhors a vacuum" is "nature abhors a blank canvas." Few, if any, surfaces, bodies, or creatures in this world don't have some pattern, some special marking to break their potential uniformity. No modern technique can create a shape, a form, a blending of colors whose prototype has not already been developed in nature.

It is from this array of patterns that we draw our impressions of the world. Although vision is an important sense to most living things, few are as sight-reliant as humans. A fox's perception of its world is developed from the scents its able nose sniffs, the sounds its sharp ears hear, and, to some degree, the images that its eyes detect. But hearing and smelling play a far smaller role in our perceptions because these senses are not as keen in humans as they are in many other animals.

Long ago, in our evolution from something much closer to apes than *Homo sapiens,* we turned from being hunters and gatherers who relied heavily on scent and sound to survive, to being agriculturalists who raise their own crops and herds which can be identified by sight. As we evolved, we no longer needed such acute senses of hearing and smell to help us evade our predators. Not only did our enemies become fewer and less fearsome, but we were able to rely on sight and intelligence to protect us from those that remained.

Humans base their perceptions primarily on images. For example, most people have stored mental pictures of the creature we call a butterfly. Perhaps a childhood recollection of the softness of the wings of a captured specimen, or of the warmth of the sun on the day it was captured, are mixed in the memory. But the primary thought is an image of what we have seen. The shapes and colors have defined the object for us.

Visual patterns in nature are the keys that help us learn about, remember, and link elements of the world around us. Once we've assimilated knowledge about a particular pattern, we can extend that knowledge to new and unfamiliar situations where that same pattern occurs.

For example, consider the coil or spiral. Most of us probably first observed this in some common backyard creature, such as

the well-armored pill bug. We poked and prodded at the insect until it curled into its "pill" posture of defense, with its segmented shell guarding it against the outside world. Perhaps we next encountered a similar shape and behavior in the millipede, again for reasons of self-defense. As our experiences grew, we could extrapolate this knowledge to an understanding of similar patterns in other creatures, such as the armadillo and the even more exotic pangolin.

Other animals rely less on such direct defense and more on the passive protection of camouflage, one of the most intriguing ways patterns in nature are manifested. Humans have demonstrated incredible ingenuity in devising new schemes to keep from being seen under a wide array of circumstances. A quick paging through any hunting supply catalog, or a trip to an army-navy surplus store, will turn up dozens of solutions to the camouflage question. However, those creations are like a lone brush stroke among the thousands that make up a finished painting when compared to the wonders that nature has worked in the area of camouflage.

Most living creatures display a binary symmetry (one half of their bodies looks like the other half) which makes it difficult for them to hide effectively without some additional help from patterning. Disruptive marking is nature's way of helping animals deal with this problem. Stripes or bands across the length or width of the animal, irregular patches across the entire body, limbs that appear to be part of the torso when held still, and shading from dark to light on portions of the body all help to disrupt the outline of an animal's form.

The spotted coat of the cheetah may not appear to offer much disruptive value when the animal is viewed in a zoo's cage, away from its natural environment. But amid the tall, dry, brown grasses of the African plains, the animal is not so easy to detect. Tigers appear similarly garish when seen under zoo conditions. However, when the big cat stalks its prey through the dense Asiatic jungles, it moves as a shadow through the alternating patches of sun and shade that mark the forest floor.

Similar striped markings have developed in many diverse

creatures. The northern pike, muskellunge, and perch of North America are all effective predators of smaller fish because of such patterning. They wait patiently, hidden among underwater vegetation that has a similar vertical alignment, then dart out of concealment to slash at their prey with toothy jaws.

On some animals, stripes have been adapted to cloak their presence from potential predators and, if that fails, to confuse the attacker. The zebra of Africa and its namesake, zebra fish—the common aquarium fish—are both covered in dark and light stripes, vertical on the equine and horizontal on the fish, and both live their lives in groups of their species.

From a distance, the stripes disrupt the outline of the animals, allowing the creatures to blend with their surroundings. When the environmental distortions common to the two species' natural habitats are considered—the rising heat radiation on the African plains and the murky liquidity of African lakes—the effect is even more marked.

And, when a predator is not fooled and investigates further, the group of zebra or zebra fish moves in unison and the striped body of each individual blends with the like stripes of those next to it. Selecting any individual for the kill thus becomes much more difficult for the would-be predator.

However, no camouflage mechanism is 100 percent foolproof. If that were the case, the earth would be entirely populated by those vegetarians that are commonly referred to as prey species. Predators would die out because they would be unable to secure their meals. Thus, no defense or attack mechanism ensures the survival of every creature that carries it. But nature, when uninterrupted by humans, generally works to allow enough members of any given species to survive and procreate.

For many bird species, adequate camouflage is the crucial key to producing each new generation. The female is often much more amply endowed with protective coloration. The hen ring-necked pheasant, for example, is a dull bird indeed next to its mate. But the hen of this species must sit for three weeks on its eggs on the ground and tend to the chicks for their first few weeks of life. The hen is much more vulnerable during this period than the fancy, strutting cock, which is off in search of its next mate.

However, among those species of birds in which the male shares the nesting and rearing duties, both genders are likely to exhibit the same protective coloring. This is evident in the monogamous snipe, for example. Both sexes carry very effective camouflage in their mottled brown-and-black plumage.

The same is generally true about males and females of nocturnal bird species that pass the daylight hours at rest. If not for their camouflage, they would be vulnerable to predation by enemies that hunt by day.

To other species, body shape and form are as important as coloration in their attempts at concealment. The aptly named walkingstick species all have the features of sticks or twigs, including various knots and crooks. As they stand on a tree or a bush, they are extremely difficult to discern.

The mantid species generally resemble the leaves and flowers of the plants that they inhabit. One species that is most commonly found among pink-purple orchids in the tropics of southeast Asia is indistinguishable from the petals of those flowers.

Leaf insects and leaf moths carry the imitation even further. The primary sections of their bodies have veins running through them, just like the leaves they frequent. Their appendages have evolved leaflike serrated edges and some even quiver like a leaf shaking in a breeze.

While these insects are colored and patterned after living plant parts, the leaf fish spends its life among dead, faded leaves that have fallen into the water. It therefore has evolved the pale, orangish yellow coloring of this debris. In addition, the skin at its mouth extends in a curve that replicates the broken stem of a leaf.

Plant parts are not the only natural objects that animals mimic. The alligator snapper turtle of North America and the rockfish look similar to stones common in their environments. The mottled, creamy gray and dull black-brown caterpillar of the viceroy butterfly appears to be a bird dropping on the twig where it rests.

Some species change their camouflage to coincide with their environments. Northern species, such as the snowshoe hare, long-tailed weasel, and ptarmigan are variations of brown during the warmer months of the year, but white in the snowy winter months.

Chameleons and anoles, or American chameleons, are known for their abilities to vary their skin coloring over an incredibly wide range of browns and greens to match their surroundings, but they do not have a monopoly on the talent. Frogs, cuttlefish, sole, dragonfly nymphs, and blossom spiders are just a few of the other creatures that can perform this feat.

However, some coloring in the animal world is intended to broadcast a creature's presence rather than conceal it. The many species of poison arrow frog, common to the tropical rain forests of Central and South America, are almost neon-bright in their various blues, reds, and greens. They do not blend into their dark jungle environment, but their patterns are just as protective as if they did. The small amphibians carry a poison so deadly that native peoples use it to coat their arrows and spears. Potential predators have been conditioned to avoid the frogs.

Similar, and more familiar, is the bright orange and black of the monarch butterfly. Although the insect is easy to spot and flutters about in a relatively lazy, slow fashion, few are taken by birds, the chief predators of butterflies. Because the butterfly's caterpillar feeds on the toxic milkweed plant, giving both the caterpillar and the butterfly a noxious taste, birds have learned to avoid them.

Other species have adapted to mimic the colors and patterns of the monarch and thus gain some measure of protection. The viceroy, for example, feeds on the leaves of willows, poplars, and various fruit trees. It gains no noxious taste from this diet. But, because of its monarchlike pattern, it too is avoided by most birds.

Predators are also fooled by the bright eyespots that many butterfly species carry on their wings. The buckeye's fore wing, for example, displays a distinct, circular "eye" that leads attacks away from the insect's vital body parts.

One thing that is obvious in many of these examples is that once nature finds something that works, be it pattern, color, shape, or form, that special something is repeated again and again. Some shapes and patterns carry across the animal, plant, and mineral sectors of the natural world and are put to use by a large number of creatures and entities for vastly different reasons. The hexagon is such a shape.

Snowflakes are one natural example of a hexagon. Nearly all snowflakes have six sides. However, no two snowflakes are exactly alike and there appears to be no end to the variations that are possible, although the differences may only be apparent under a microscope. Depending upon the temperature at which the ice crystals form, everything from flat, platelike designs to needle-like columns to fern-leafed stars is possible.

The hexagon is also a common shape among mineral crystals. Calcite, arsenic, and graphite naturally occur in this shape—a visible expression of these minerals' atomic structures.

Although the individual-to-individual details vary much less than among snowflakes, honeycombs feature another six-sided natural shape. Created by honeybees as they construct their combs, each one of the thousands of beeswax cells that make up a comb is hexagonal. A shape with six sides is not a chance occurrence. As a separate structure, each cell is weak and fragile. But interlocked with all the other cells, a great strength is achieved by the compensating opposite but equal pressures that push toward the center of each hexagonal cell.

Hexagons are also utilized in other ways in the insect world. The compound eyes of these creatures are made up of tiny hex-agonal facets called *ommatidia*. The number of these units in the insect eye varies greatly, from just nine in some ants that never come out of their underground chambers, to more than 30,000 in fast-flying dragonflies.

Many crustaceans, such as crabs, share the six-sided facet characteristic in their compound eyes. However, some, like shrimp, lobster, and crayfish, have adapted square-faceted eyes with mirrorlike chambers beneath them to present a brighter image to their brains.

Circles, and their three-dimensional manifestations, spheres, are also seen again and again throughout nature, beginning with our greatest sphere, the earth, which is actually somewhat flattened at the North and South poles. A circular shape appears in phenomena such as whirlpools, tornadoes, and hot springs because of the rotation of the earth. The circle and sphere shapes are also utilized in things ranging from the image-gathering eyeball to the growth rings of a tree trunk.

Horns and antlers are another oft-repeated fixture in the natural world. Members of the deer, antelope, and cattle families come immediately to mind. But the defensive, and, during the mating season offensive, projections are also seen quite commonly in the reptile world, in species such as the horned lizards, and in the insect kingdom, in species such as the antlered treehopper and the stag beetle.

The elements, too, contribute to the earth's incredible array of patterns. Ice, for example, assumes a myriad of forms ranging from flat sheet ice, crystal clear and unblemished; to hoar frost that coats tree limbs in a confectionary-like whiteness; to massive frozen cascades of tints and hues draping on the sheer face of a cliff.

In its glacial form, ice—from the last Ice Age, 10,000 to 15,000 years ago—has created fields of polished boulders where no trees grow in the eastern United States and the "knife-sliced" granite sides of the majestic Yosemite Valley in the West, among many other phenomena.

Ice in its liquid form, water, offers us many variations on the S-curve as it meanders through the great rivers of the world. One of the most awe-inspiring landmarks on the face of the earth, the mile-deep Grand Canyon, is the result of such slow but tireless action by water. At the very bottom of the canyon is the Colorado River, which continues wearing away at the rock. But en route from the lip of the canyon to the river is the story of how the earth's surface developed. Like a rainbow of rock, the walls of the canyon pass from red and yellowish brown sandstone to greenish shale to grayish red limestone, and finally, at the lowest exposed level, to black rock known as *schist*.

Another oft-repeated pattern of nature is the wrinkle and crack evidenced in the dry, fissured earth that was once the bottom of a mud puddle, or the radiating rays of tiny hairline fractures in an iced-over pond, or even the cracks in the sidewalk.

Everywhere on earth, natural forces constantly cause cracks and wrinkles, from the folded outcroppings of rocks in the Titus Canyon of Death Valley to the folds of skin encircling an elephant's legs in the African bush. These curving, snagging lines are an indication of the one constant that nature forces upon everything on earth: change. Cracking ice signals changing temperature. Cracking rock bespeaks a new topography being created for that part of the globe. Wrinkled elephant skin signifies the aging of the magnificent beast.

Like cracks, sand dunes on beaches and in deserts across the globe have seemingly random patterns. But, closer inspection reveals that a few forms do occur with regularity and do, indeed, dominate these sandy environments.

Crescent shapes, with ends pointing downwind, are common where hard and flat surfaces exist beneath the sand. In those areas where there is little vegetation to deflect the winds, cavelike dunes may form perpendicular to the wind direction. U-shaped dunes sometimes form on the downwind side of older, long-standing dunes as the latter begin to disintegrate and new sand begins to collect at their edges. Where sand is relatively limited and winds tend to blow in primarily one direction year-round, ridgelike structures may form parallel to the prevailing gusts.

These same patterns are often repeated in the sky, where winds push and move and shape the collection of airborne water droplets called clouds into an ever-changing array of shape and form. As meteorologists and most practiced outdoorspeople know, different cloud types are generally associated with certain types of weather.

Altocumulus clouds are thin and cottony and may stretch in puffs for long distances. They are usually accompanied by clear, settled weather. *Stratocumuli* are thick, ball-like clouds that gather into large masses that fill the sky overhead. They forecast changing weather and precipitation.

Nimbostratus are those dark gray sheets of clouds whose arrival signals the coming of rain or snow. *Cumulonimbus* clouds form as tall, white towers, with an almost wavelike appearance, to forecast the coming of harsh weather, such as thunderstorms. The scattered and stretched wisps of white clouds known as *cirrus* generally signal a period of fine weather.

Caused by the same winds, waves take on many of the same shapes as clouds and sand dunes, although in a much more fleeting way. When the wind pushes down on the surface on the water, waves take form. When wind blows behind those waves, they grow into much larger waves. And, when still stronger winds push so hard that the wave tops are blown free, the waves become whitecaps.

In turn, the waves create a profile on the shoreline where they eventually crash. Elements of these coastal profiles generally include the wave-cut cliff, the more gently sloping wave-cut beach, the beach of sediment washed about by the waves, and the wave-built terrace of sediment extending out from the breaker area. In addition, a rocky coast will have sea caves, sea arches, and stacks created as the waves tear away at the bedrock of the shore.

Similar crevices, cracks, and openings are on display elsewhere as well. Thousands of years of erosion and weathering have carved tall spires from the soft sandstone in Utah's Bryce Canyon, just as thousands of years of dripping, calcareous water has built stalagmites up from the floors of caves across the globe. Thus, gravity exerts its influence in seemingly opposite directions but with similar effect and pattern.

A like shape is achieved in the animal world, in the pinnaclelike columns constructed by termites in Africa and Australia. The pinnacles, which can rise many feet from the ground, are formed by the insects carrying tiny bits of earth from underground and cementing them in place with body fluids.

A visual foil to pinnacles and stalagmites, icicles and stalactites are formed by water and gravity. As water drips off a surface in cold weather, it freezes and gradually grows into an icicle. Water likewise drips off the roof of a cave, but this water is rich with limestone leached from rock. It also forms into a hanging, spearlike point as each water drop dries and leaves behind the limestone.

Other types of water-borne accumulations are also possible. The white limestone formations in areas such as Yellowstone National Park's Mammoth Hot Springs bear a striking resemblance to the large fields of ice that make up glaciers. The terraces at Mammoth are constructed as calcium carbonate dissolved from limestone beneath the surface is carried upward in rising hot water and exposed. Glaciers are formed as snow collects in a depression, each new layer applying pressure on the one below it and compacting it into ice. Eventually the pressure becomes great enough to force out a branch of ice, which is the beginning of the glacier. This same glacial look is recreated in caves across the globe, as calcite-rich water forms what is known as *flowstone*.

The feather is another shape that has evolved in many different creatures for many different reasons. On birds, of course, lightweight feathers provide insulation and water-proofing and help the bird to fly. There are many different types of bird feathers: contour feathers, which provide the outer contour of the bird and are the key to flight; semiplumes, which offer a measure of insulation, flexibility at joints, and some buoyancy (in water birds); down, which is the main insulator; filoplumes, which transmit signals from the outer contour feathers to the skin; and powder feathers, which don't even resemble feathers and function in the bird's preening procedures.

The feather pattern is put to use quite differently in other living things. The feathery hydroid, which looks like a bird's feather that is soaking wet, uses its floating tentacles to snag and sting its passing prey from the waters of its subtropical Atlantic home. Ferns also are commonly described as feathery in appearance, a form they use to gather as much sunlight as possible from the shady environments in which they generally grow.

Like the fern which resembles one aspect of the animal world, so too do some sea creatures resemble aspects of the plant world. Many sea anemones have a distinctly floral look to them, although the resemblance is closer to many other types of flowers than to their land-based namesake. The "flower petals" of the sea anemones are actually tentacles that surround the orifice and grasp, paralyze, and place in the mouth any prey that swims by. Most species tend to contract the tentacles when danger threatens.

Some species of coral, which are also tiny marine animals, likewise share patterns with terrestrial life. Precious coral could pass for apple tree branches in miniature, staghorn coral for the branches of a frosted fir tree, and leaf coral for a crisp head of iceberg lettuce. Present in the marine world, too, is the brain coral.

Of course, some natural patterns, shapes, and color schemes are without equal. One such phenomenon is the aurora, which manifests itself in the northern hemisphere as the *aurora borealis*, or northern lights. A similar phenomenon occurring in the southern hemisphere is called the *aurora australis.*

An aurora is an otherworldly display of lights and colors in the night sky over polar regions that can be seen thousands of miles away. Photographs only begin to capture the full beauty of the seemingly endless array of forms that the light assumes, although the most common are clouds and ribbons.

Comprising the aurora are rapidly shifting patches and columns of light of every color imaginable. High-energy atomic particles emitted from sunspots are the trigger for the glow. Therefore, the most intense auroras occur just after peaks in the sunspot cycle and are accompanied by disturbances in magnetic forces and radio waves here on earth.

Rainbows are another unmatchable light show. Most often seen in the sky after a rain shower or in the mist of waterfalls, the arching effect is caused by sunlight reflecting from drops of water falling through the air. Rainbows are visible only when the angle of reflection between the observer, the water drops, and

the sun is between 40 and 45 degrees.

The area of the American Southwest called the Painted Desert is unmatched for the magnitude of its grandeur. In this choice place, which stretches for more than 200 miles northwest to southeast and ranges in width from 15 to 30 miles, century upon century of erosion by wind and rain have exposed ancient layers of rock.

Sandstone, shale, and clay dating to the Permian and Triassic periods display their layers of pink, purple, brown, gray, white, yellow, and blue—all dominated by brilliant red—in the mesas, escarpments, and hills that seem to extend forever. The incredibly clear atmosphere, even in today's polluted world, and the intense rays of the desert sun combine to drive the overall effect of the myriad hues and shades to unbelievable heights of beauty.

Petrified trees also display unique patterns. Occurring at many locations across the earth, they are the remains of trees that lived millions of years ago. When they died, they were covered by sediment. As water penetrated their structures, silica and other minerals replaced the wood fibers, and the trees were gradually converted to stone. The minerals, such as carbon, iron, and manganese, lent their own colors to the easily stained silica to create brilliant coloring in the stone casts of the wood fibers.

One of the largest groupings of such trees lies in eastern Arizona's Petrified Forest National Park. A half-dozen different forests of the trees have been unearthed, which include some trees that measure six feet in diameter and more than 100 feet in length.

From these very unique instances to the common and widely employed designs, nature offers what at first glance appears to be a totally random array of patterns and colors. However, for those who are willing to take the time to really see, there is a rhythm, a constant re-use of patterns, to be discovered. But even a lifetime would not be enough to capture them all. And there lies the crux of our constant fascination with them.

SUBLIME COINCIDENCES

*T*hroughout nature, certain color combinations and shapes are repeated over and over again. Sometimes this repetition occurs for very functional reasons, but at other times it is simply by coincidence—a sort of natural accident that delights the observer and sparks a desire to find other matching patterns and shapes in far-reaching and diverse environments.

Similarities can occur in creatures or objects from the animal, vegetable, and mineral worlds. For example, an open flower blossom and a sea anemone have a strikingly similar appearance. As a matter of fact, it was the marine animal's close resemblance to the anemone flower that resulted in its name.

"Eyes" appear on many animals and plants without giving them any vision at all, such as the eyespots on the wings of a moth or the knot on the side of a tree. Stripes, too, such as those on the zebra and its namesake, the zebra fish, are also commonly repeated.

Mushroom edges, San Mateo County, California

Leaves of the kalanchoe, a South African succulent

Gerbera daisy blossom

Into the mouth of a Pacific Northwest coast sea anemone

A passionflower growing in central Texas

Cross section of the interior of a chambered nautilus shell

A desert millipede in protective coiled posture

California poppy

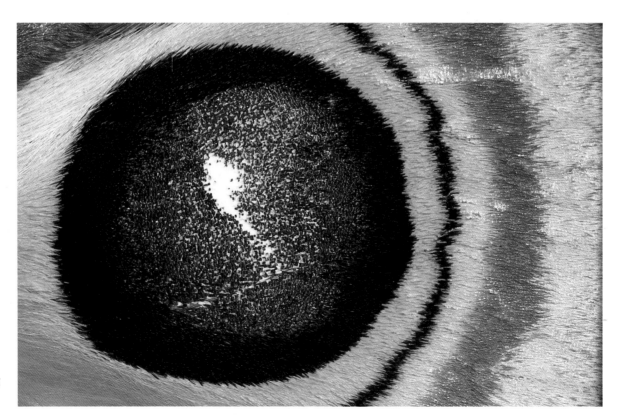

The eyespot on a moth's wing

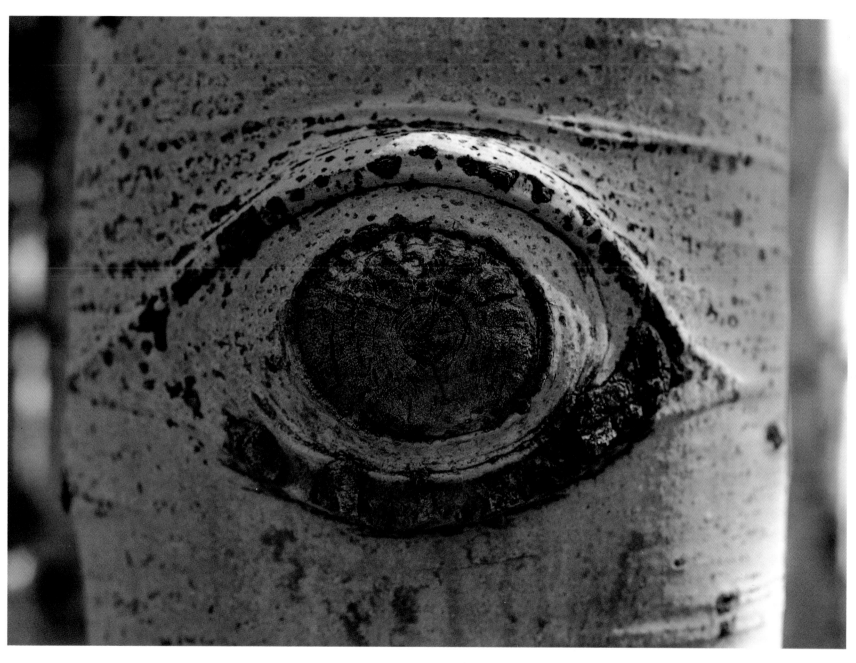

Gnarl on the trunk of a white birch tree

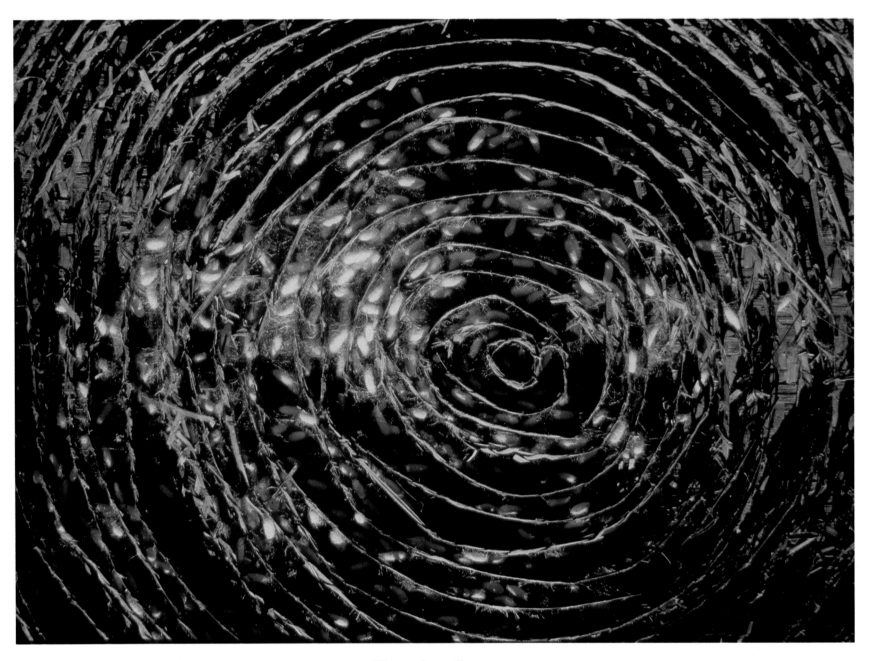

Silk spun by a silkworm

Weather-worn wood

Cracked, alkaline floor of Death Valley, California Opposite: *A honeycomb* Insert: *Black basalt columns of the Giant's Causeway, County Derry, Northern Ireland*

Reversing Falls at St. John, New Brunswick, Canada

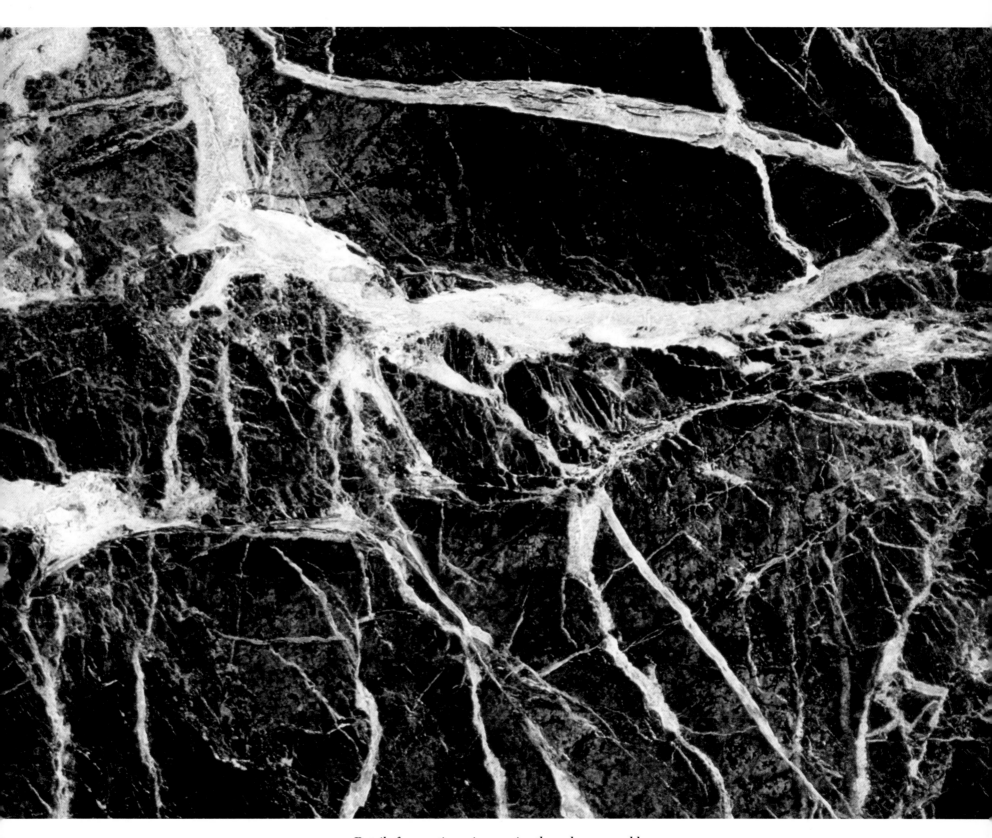

Detail of serpentine veins running through gray marble

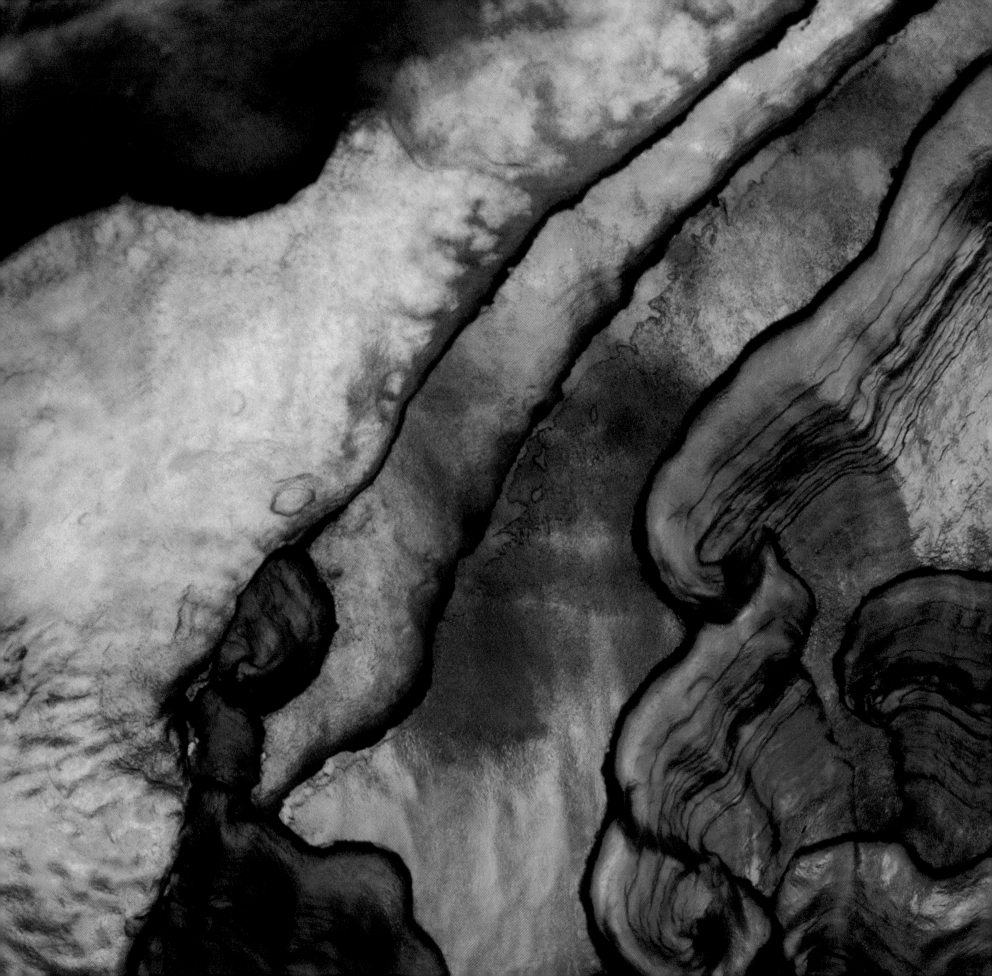

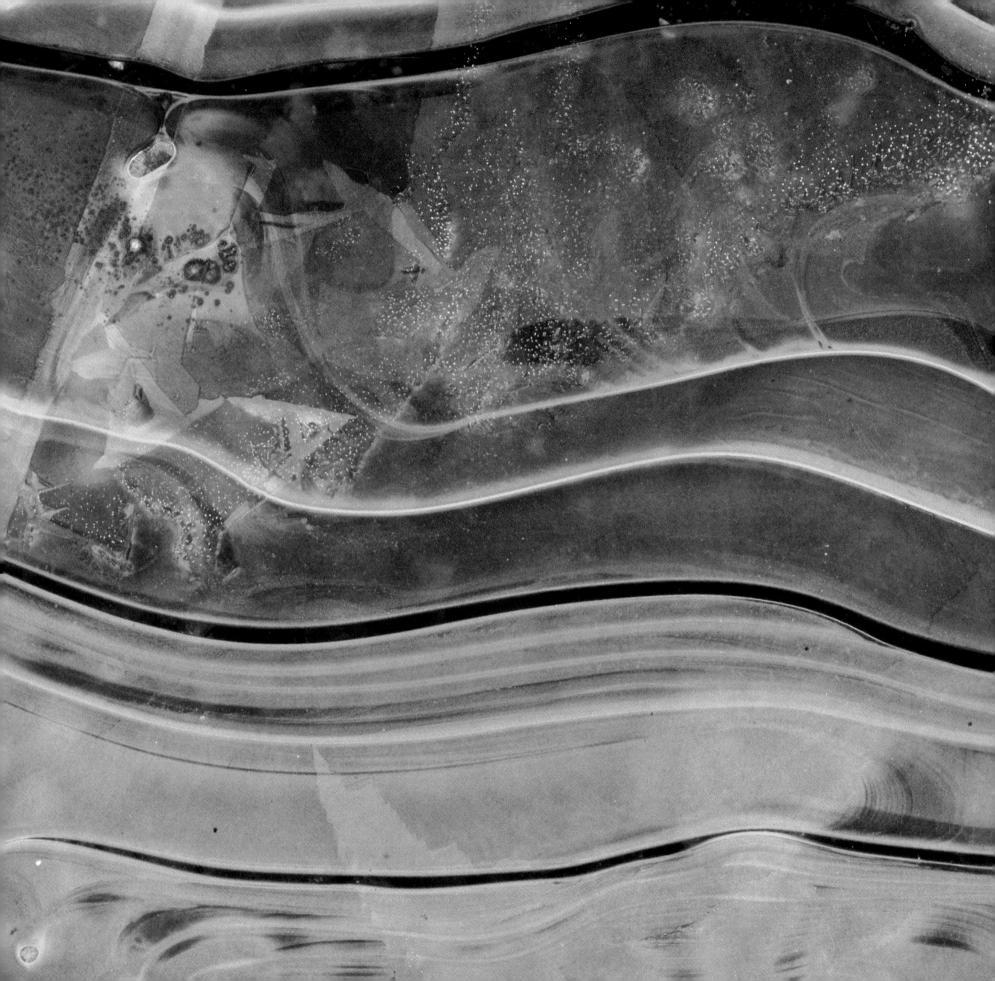

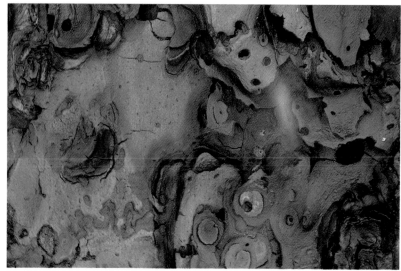

Preceding pages: *An abalone shell interior* Left: *Thin layer of ice over a stream near Harrowsmith, Ontario, Canada* Above: *Peeling bark of an Everglades tree*

A mass of bloodworms, commonly used as live bait

Close-up of a cluster of brain coral in the Florida Keys

Gorgonians, invertebrate animals, in the waters of the South Pacific off Fiji

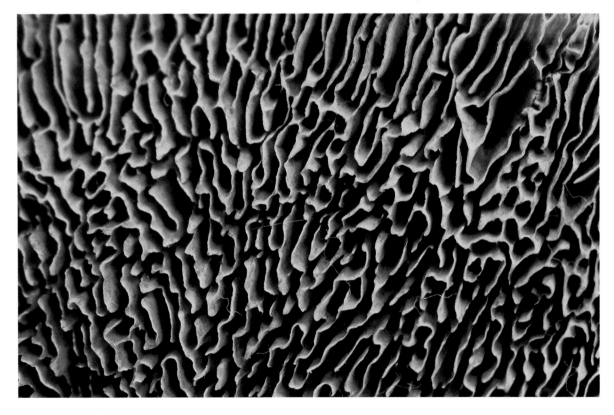

Pores of the daedalea, a large shelflike fungi that grows on oak stumps and logs

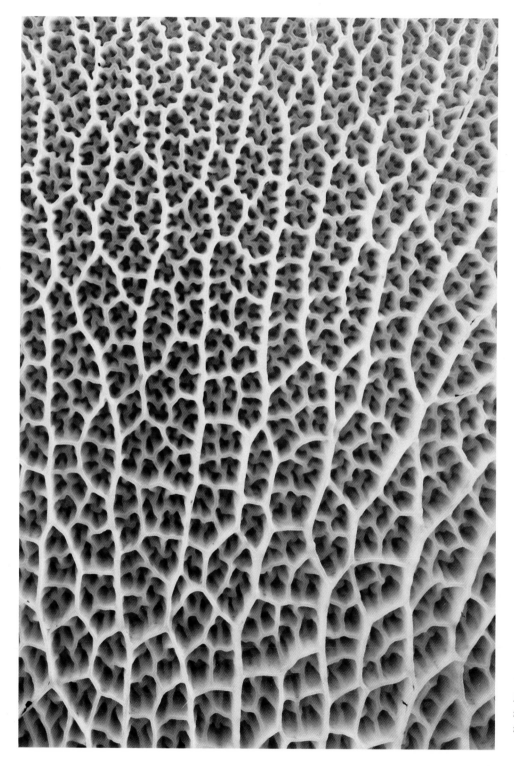

Close-up of a sea fan, an invertebrate animal of the oceans

Detail of an ash-tree bolete, a mushroom that grows near ash or maple trees

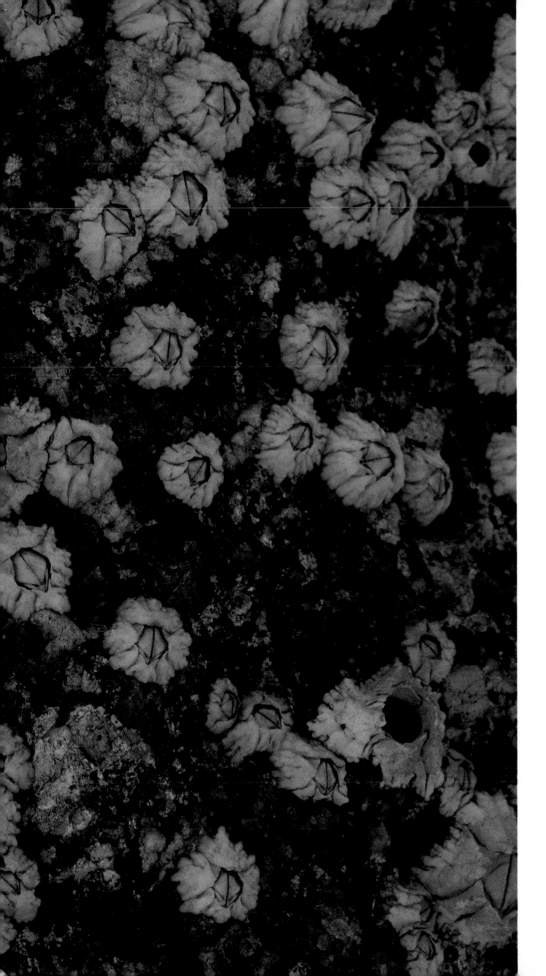

Barnacles growing on a rock in salt water
Above: Arctic forget-me-nots, Denali
National Park, Alaska

*Detail of frost on a glass
windowpane*

Palm fronds

Dry pine needles floating on still water

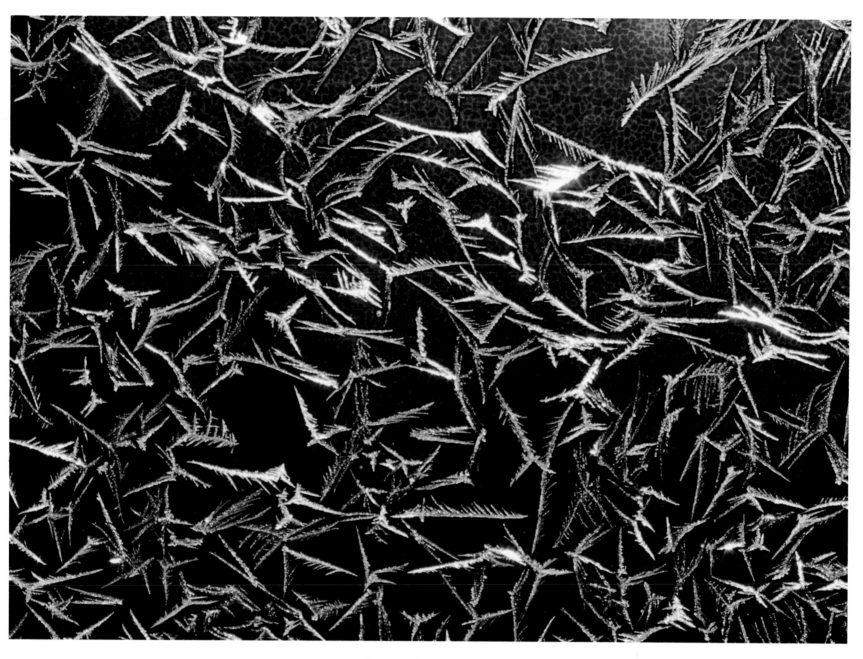

Ice crystals on a window

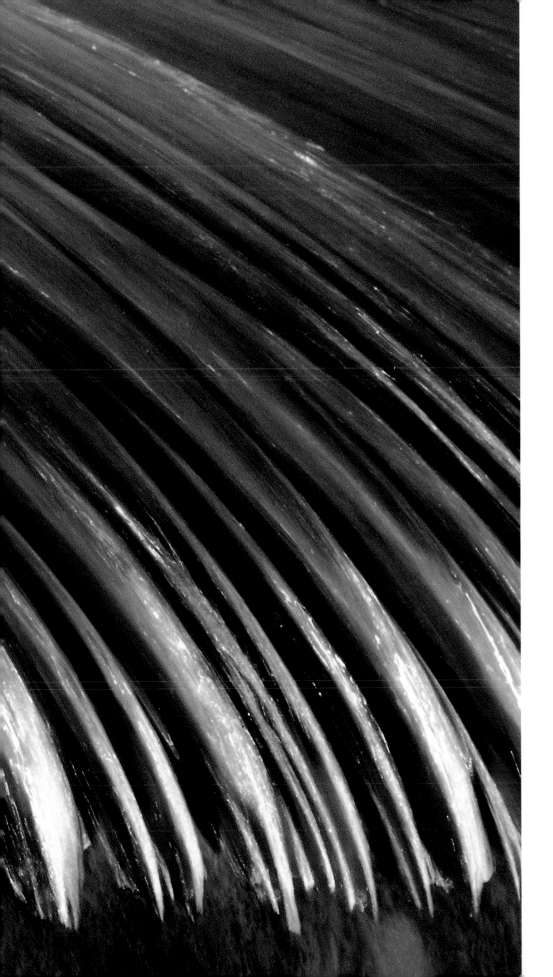

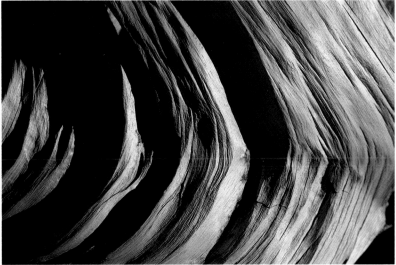

Striated ice formation Above: The weathered trunk of a whitebark pine tree at the timberline of Mt. Hood, Oregon

A moving leaf mantis among the leaves of a tropical plant

A dead-leaf mantis living in the litter on a tropical forest floor

BEGUILING DISGUISES

*I*n the chain of life, one living thing eats another living thing and is in turn eaten by yet another. In this continuous cycle of predator and prey, an intricate part of the overall scheme is the natural camouflage with which many creatures have been equipped.

Some are able to survive because they blend into their surroundings almost to the point of disappearing. Some, like the famous chameleon, or anole, can change the color of their skin to match their environments. Others, like many fish and birds, rely on patterned fur, scales, or feathers to break up their outlines as they hover near a rock, a tree, or in tall grasses. There are also those strange and mysterious creatures like the walkingstick and the rockfish, which closely resemble inanimate elements of the world around them.

Rather than blending in, still other creatures exhibit startling colors to announce that they carry a poison or foul taste or odor, while another group simply hides by looking quite like those with poison or foul taste or odor.

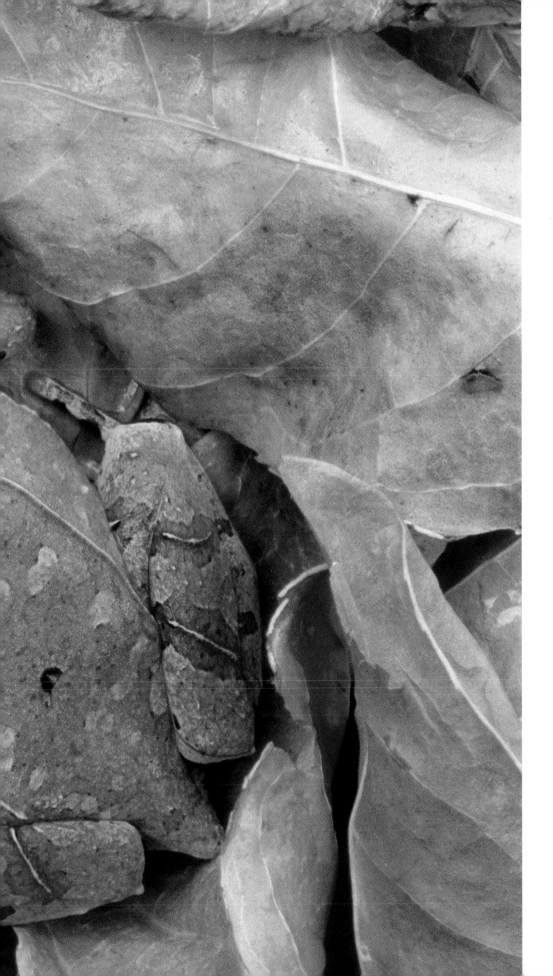

Asian leaf toad, Malaysia Above: *Asian horned toad in Malaysia*

Cluster of monarch butterflies on a tree trunk in their wintering grounds of central Mexico

A viceroy in Wakulla Springs, Florida

Walkingstick near Portal, Arizona

Walkingstick in Argentina
**Overleaf: *Summer plumage of a
white-tailed ptarmigan, which is
mostly white in winter***

A tokay, a Malaysian gecko, assumes coloring close to the branch on which it rests

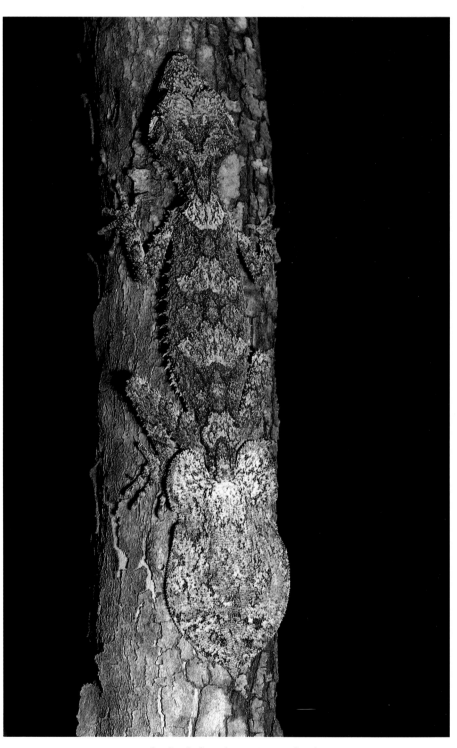

A leaf-tailed gecko in Queensland, Australia Opposite: A Peringuey's viper, mostly buried in the sands of Africa's Namib Desert

A Pacific sand dab concealed among the gravel of its ocean floor home

A sand dab's shadow betrays the fish's presence

A menacing moray eel in the Sea of Cortez

The well-camouflaged and venomous scorpion fish of the Red Sea

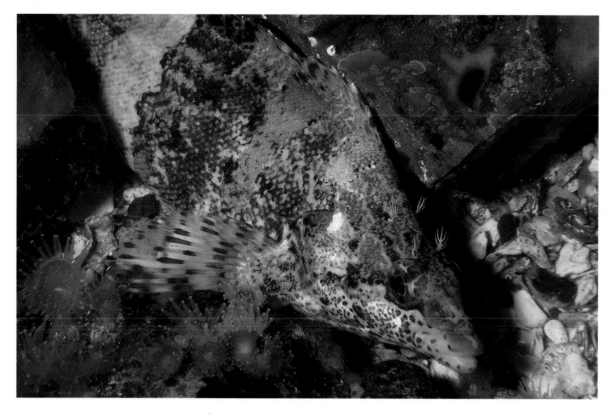

*A painted greenling in Monterey
Bay, California*

*A sculpin in its tidal pool home,
Monterey Bay, California
Following page: A Moses' sole
flounder in the Red Sea*

Close-up of the strange, asymmetrical body of a flounder

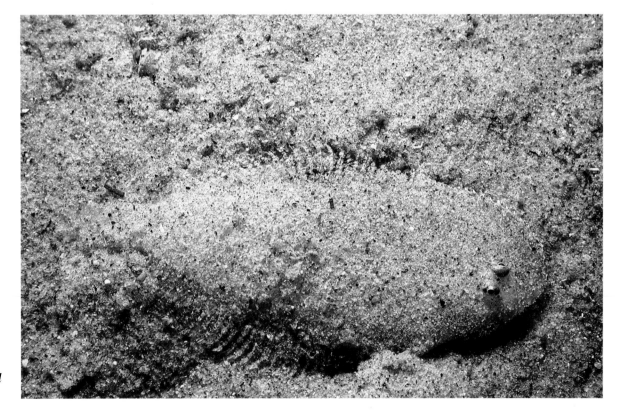

Moses' sole flounder hidden in sand

Horntail wasp in the high plains region of Texas

A wasp-mimicking moth

Pink orchids Above: An orchid mantis of the Malaysian rain forest

Close-up of a gazania blossom in California

ELEMENTAL GEOMETRY

*T*hink back to high-school geometry or grade-school art classes and pick any shape or pattern you learned there. Chances are nearly certain that you will find the shape or pattern that you called to mind somewhere in nature. Every shape that people can create or study, even in today's high-tech world of computer graphics, has already been put to use by nature—generally many times over.

Spheres appear in the fruit of many plants, as well as in rocks and in the ball-shaped cocoons spun by some insects. Hexagons show up in the honeybee's nest, in snowflakes, and in basalt rock. Lines can be found anywhere from a row of ants to cracks in ice or rock. Circles appear in the growth rings of trees, in spider's webs, and in the concentric circles formed in a pond after a bird dives below the surface. And of course, clouds, waves, and sand all sometimes form patterns of geometric shapes. In a limitless world, there is a never-ending variety of ways in which two- and three-dimensional shapes can be utilized.

Preceding pages: *Saw palmetto fronds* Above: *Developing seeds of a sunflower*

Spiral of a growing begonia leaf

Stem and leaves of a South Asian costus

The feathery leaves of a resam fern in the Malaysian rain forest

Heliconia flower, South America

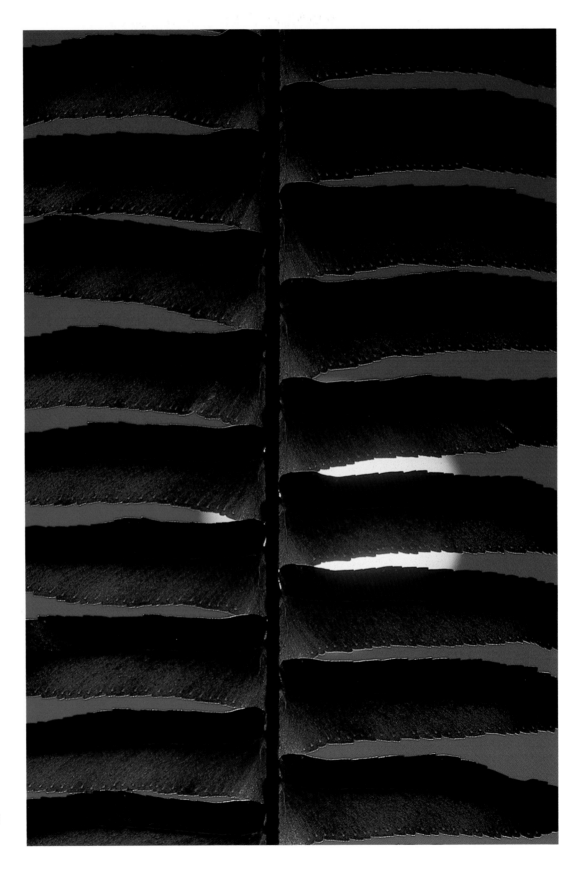

Sun outlining a fern frond

Symmetrical leaflets of a fern

Water droplets on lupines on a foggy morning Above: The deadly blossom of the carrion flower

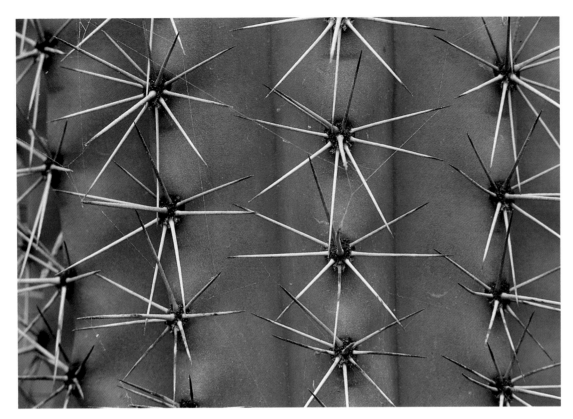

The needles of a saguaro cactus in New Mexico

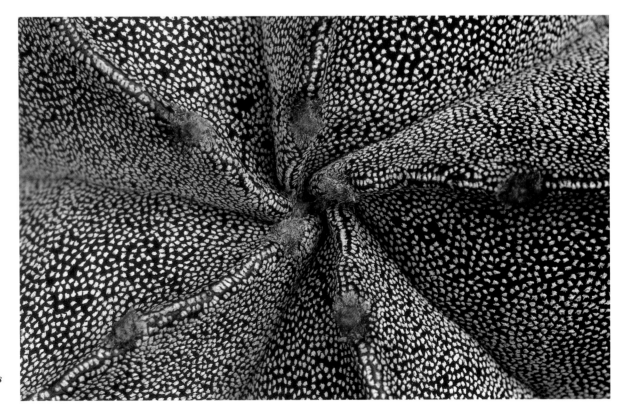

Close-up of the skin of a cactus

A pair of cobalt sea stars

Microscopic view of snowflakes

Giant green sea anemone colored by the mutualistic algae that live on its surface

Plumed seedpods of a false dandelion

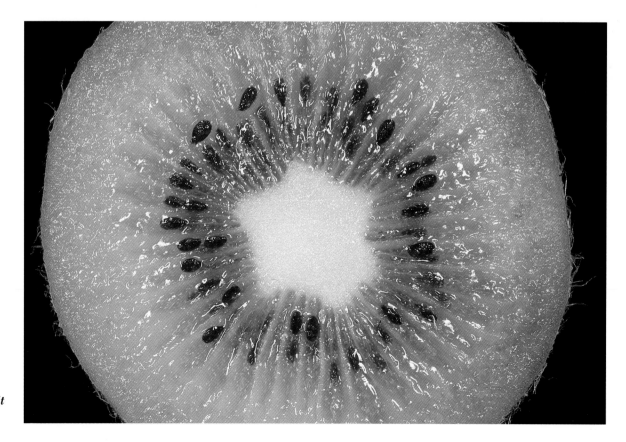

Cross section of a kiwi fruit

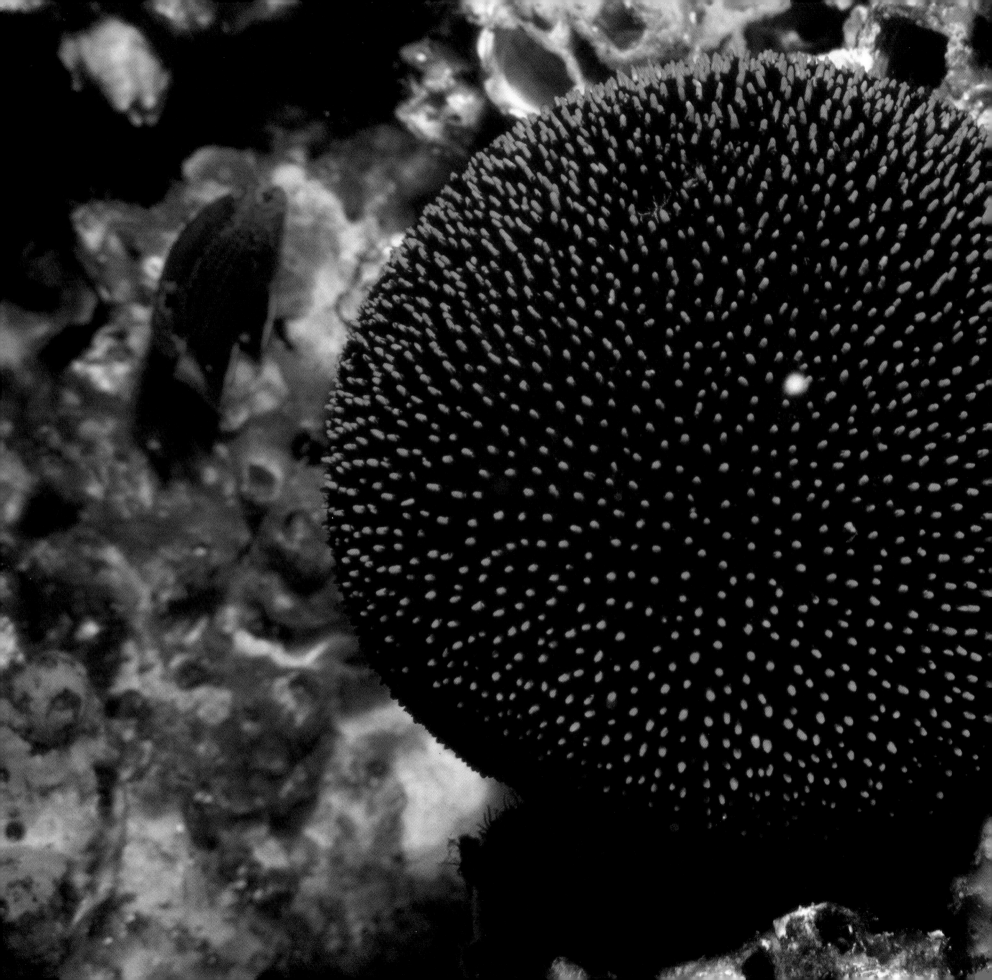

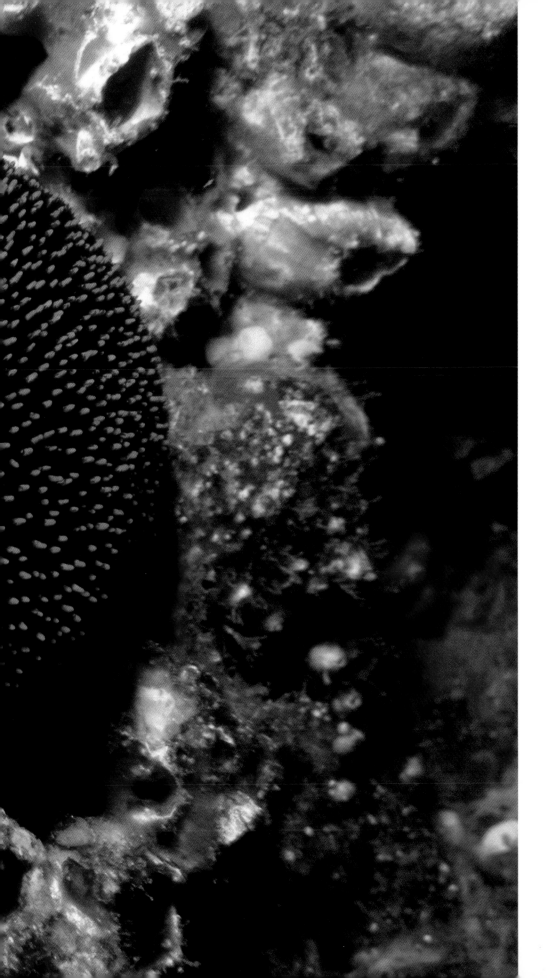

Domestar, a marine invertebrate Above:
Blossom of the eucalyptus tree

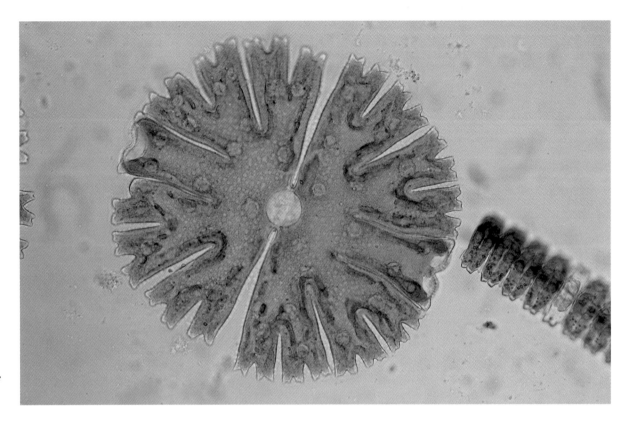

Microscopic view of green algae

Peas with the pod removed

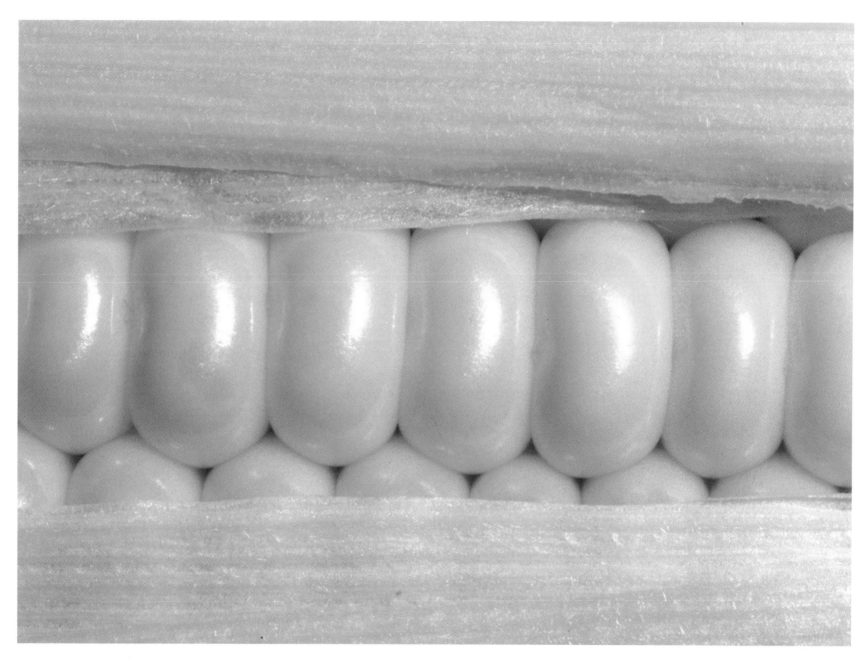

Exposed sweet corn kernels

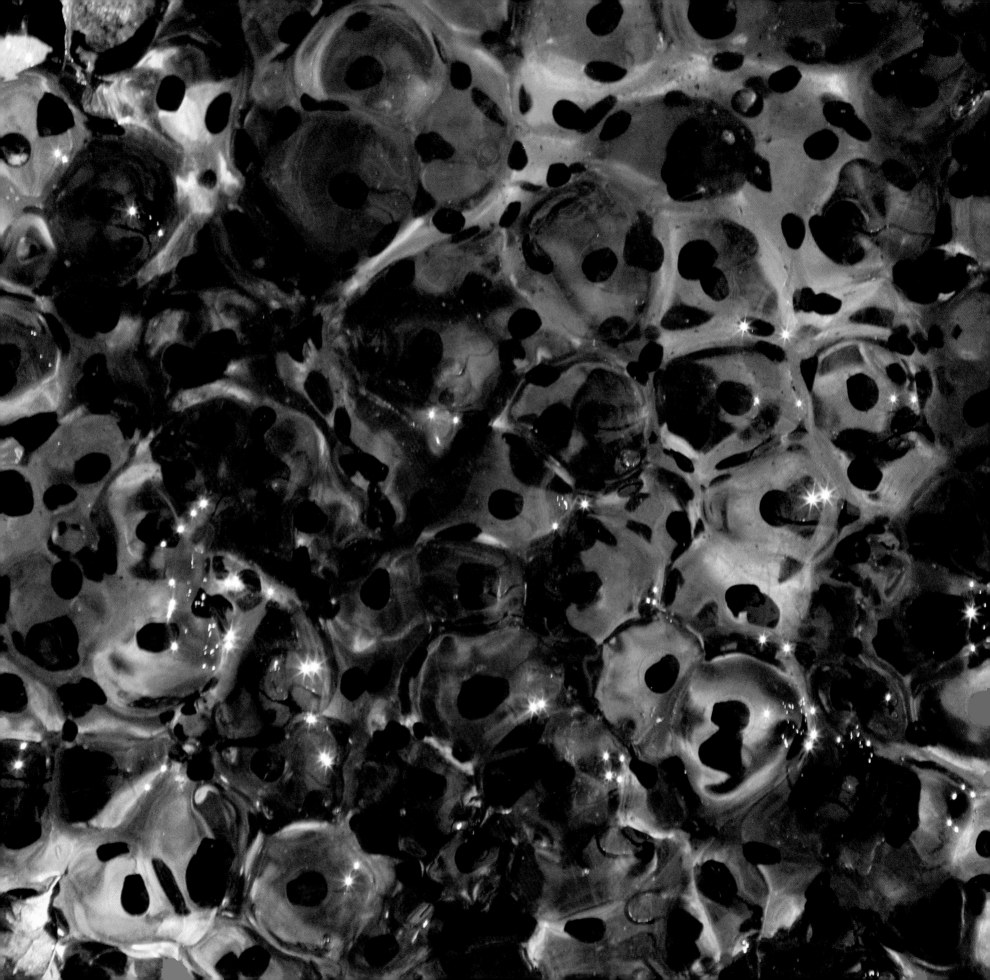

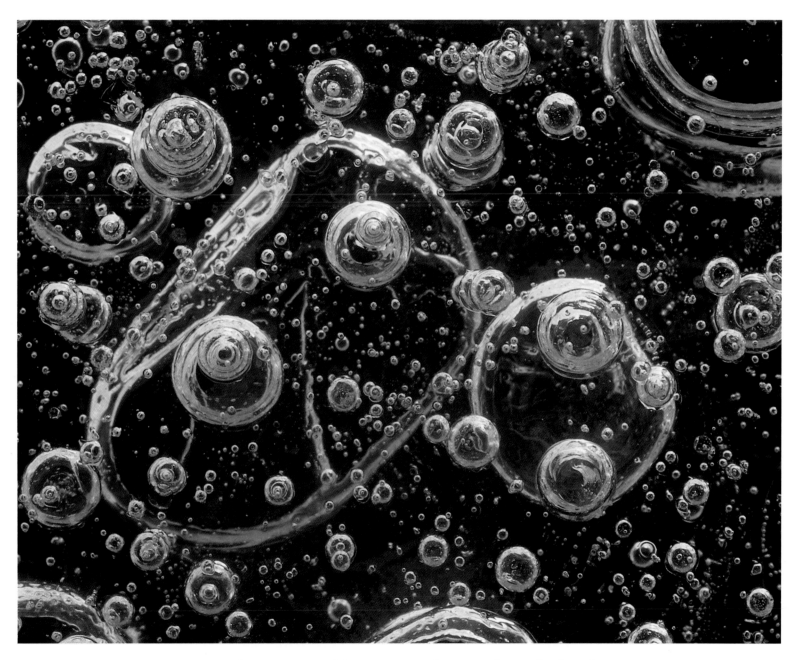

Preceding page: *A wood frog egg mass in the waters of a woodland pond*
Above: *Air bubbles encased in ice that formed over moving water*

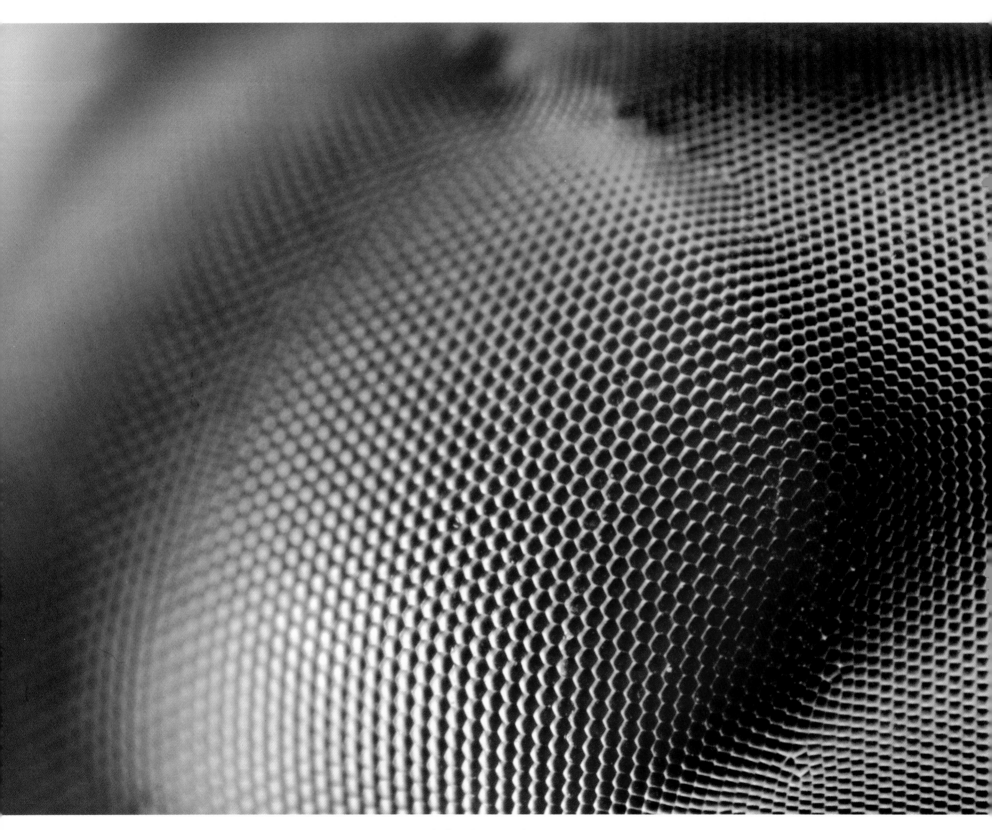

Magnified surface of a dragonfly's eye

Condensation

Parched bottom of a pond during severe drought in Australia

Dried and cracked mud

94

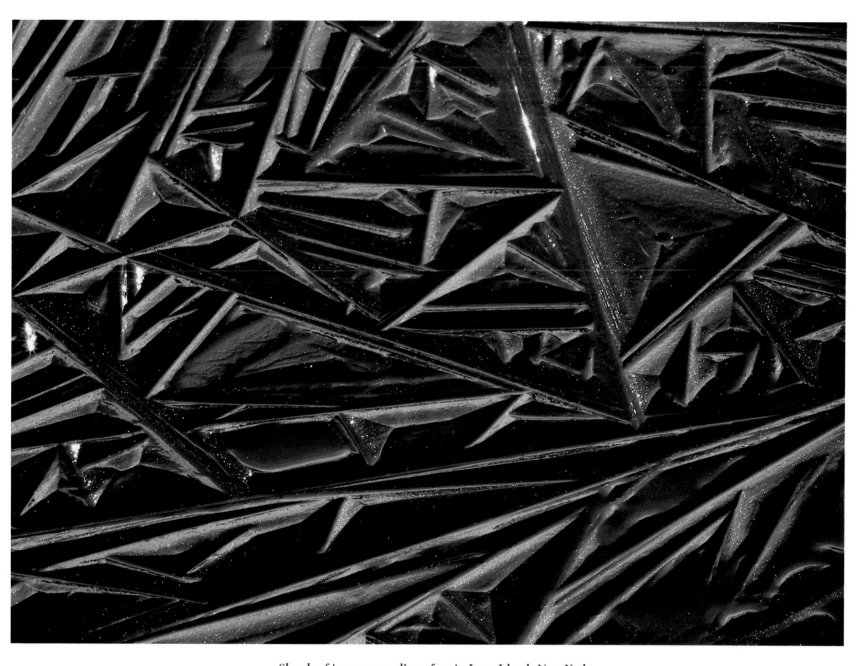

Shards of ice on a pond's surface in Long Island, New York

Preceding page: *Pattern formed by wind in a Texas sand dune* Insert: *Ocean crestline* Left: *Close-up of a primary feather of a bald eagle*

Dunes in Africa's Sahara Desert

NATURE'S MOTIFS

The elements—wind, rain, sleet, snow, ice, fire, and the like— can be harsh and devastating in their fury. But they are also part of nature's incredible array of artistic tools, able to carve magnificent panoramas from simple earth.

Any listing of famous landmarks will most certainly include a generous sampling of the works of these elements: the Grand Canyon, the Rocky Mountains, the Giant's Causeway, the Sahara Desert, Mt. Aetna . . . the list goes on and on.

Although nature's grandeur manifests itself in these awesome sites, it is also evident in more ephemeral displays, such as foaming rows of clouds, the delicate arch of a rainbow, the cracked earth of a dry streambed, the lacy crystals of snow.

It is these small treasures—the clouds that gather into a familiar shape, the ice feathers that decorate a window—which are most readily observed by people in their everyday lives, adding an element of beauty that sensitizes us to the wonder surrounding us.

Delicate arch in Arches National Park, Utah

Canyon walls worn by time and the elements in Zion National Park, Utah

Rock spires called hoodoos, Bryce Canyon, Utah

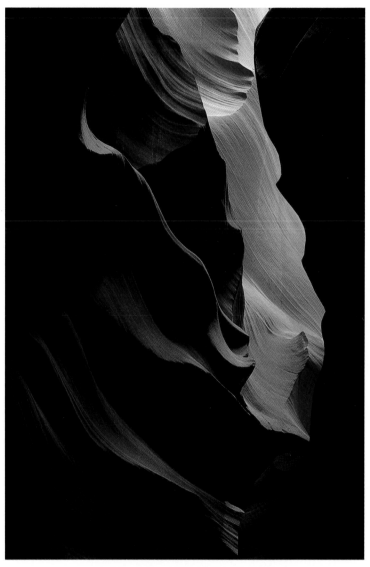

*Eroded rock walls of Sandstone Slot
Canyon, Arizona Above: Surrealistic
interior view of Sandstone Slot Canyon
Overleaf: Caps of the chicken mushroom*

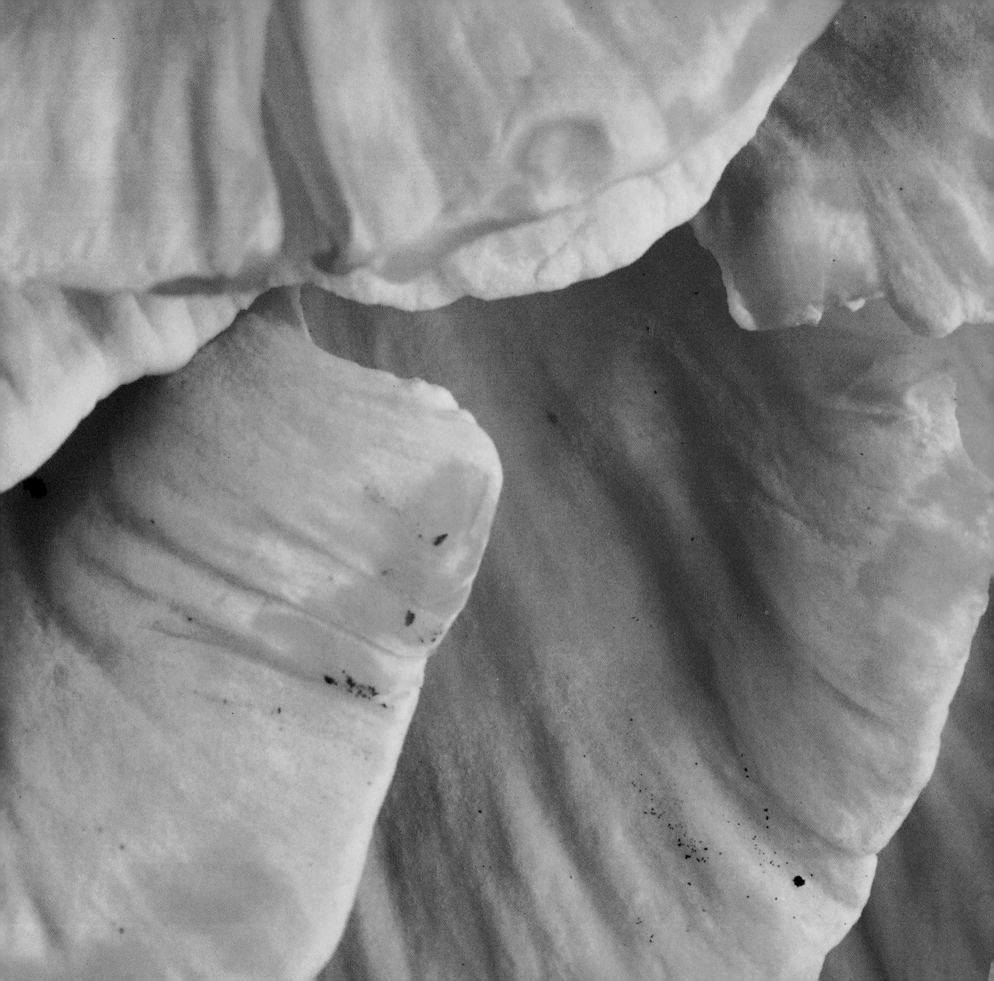

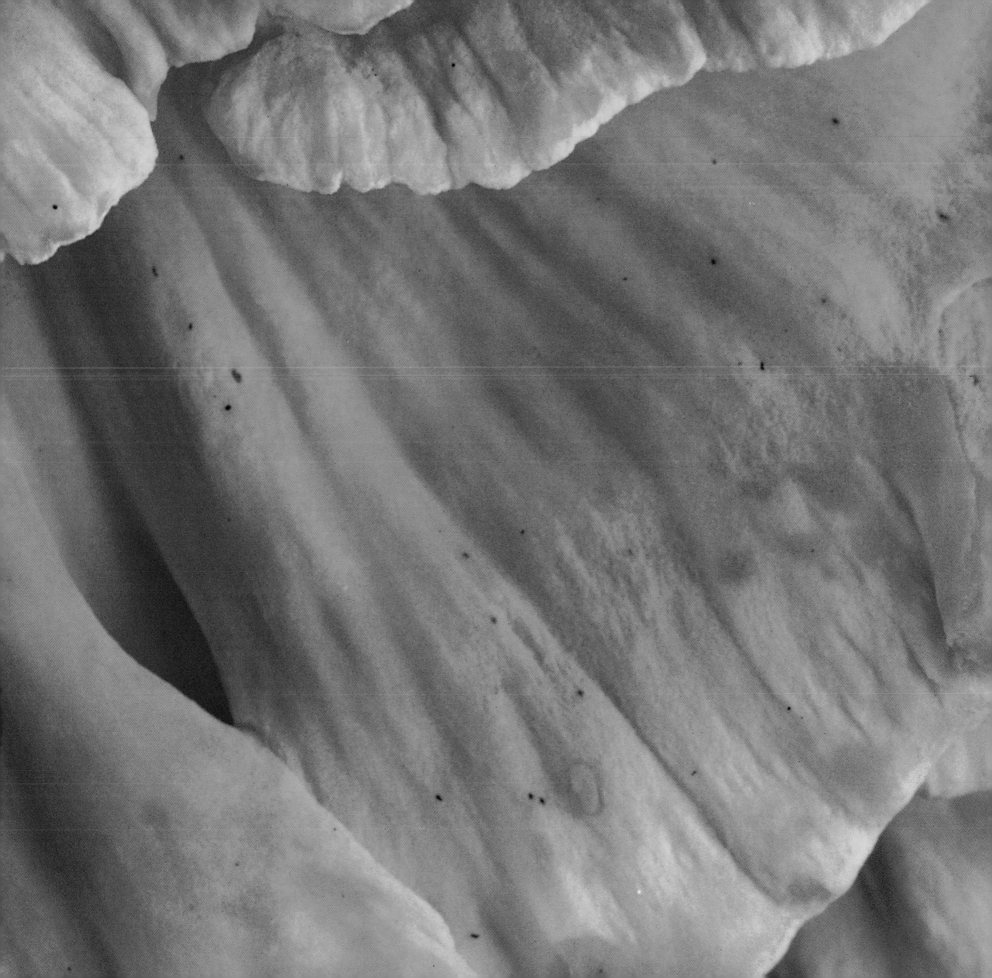

Preceding pages: *Rainbow reflected on the surface of a lagoon* Opposite: *Glowing lava of Sicily's Mt. Aetna* Left: *Icy cold runoff from the Myradalisjokvil Glacier in Iceland*

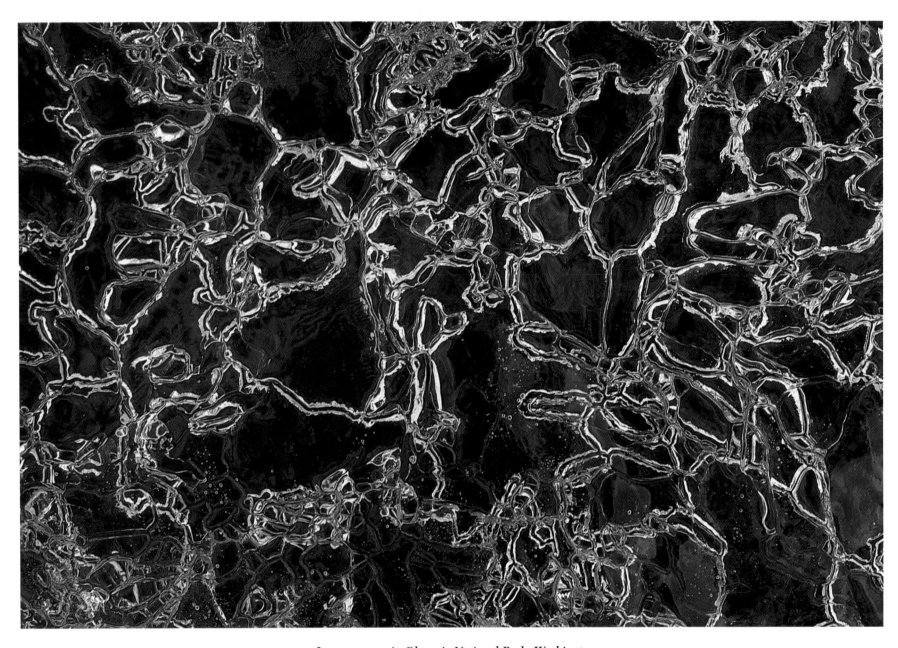

Ice on stream in Olympic National Park, Washington

Lightning striking mountains during a severe electrical storm Overleaf: *Black volcanic sand tints the ice of an Icelandic glacier*

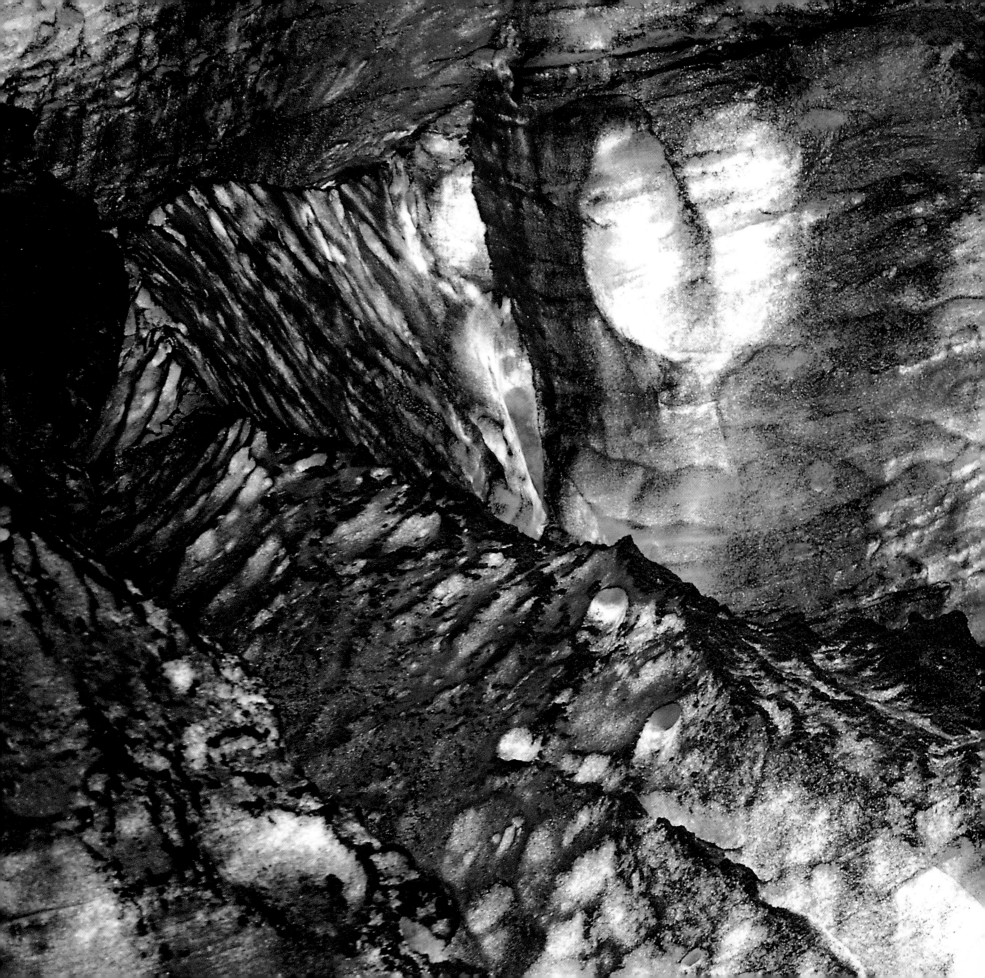

Dew on the web of an orb-weaving spider

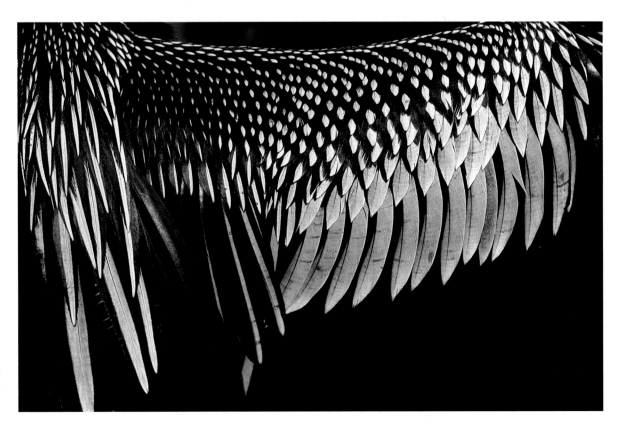

The wing of an anhinga in Everglades National Park, Florida

Stripes of a Hartmann's mountain zebra

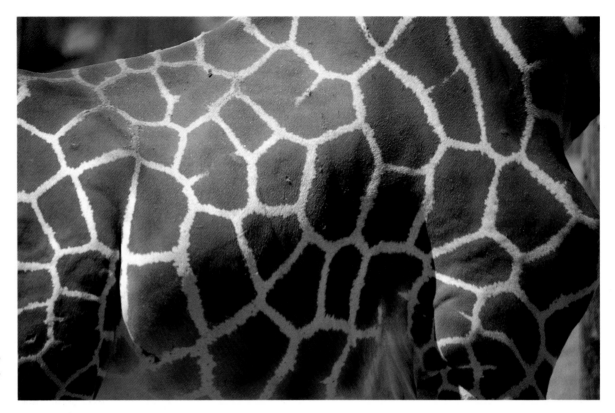

The exotic markings on the side of a giraffe

Luxuriously spotted coat of the ocelot

Iridescent breast feathers of a cock ring-necked pheasant

Chinese lantern plant silhouetted by a setting sun

Veins of a prayer plant leaf

Autumn leaves cover the surface of a pond

Young leaves of an ornamental cabbage

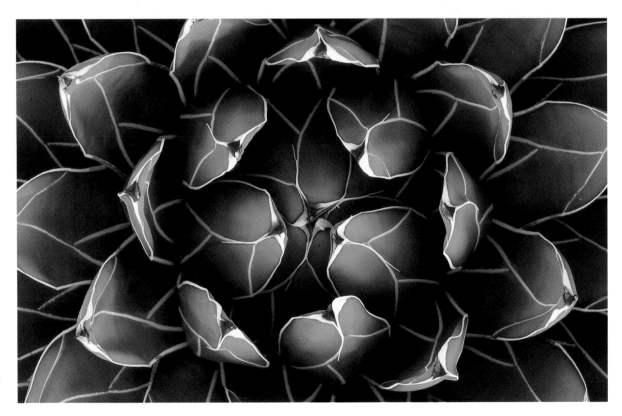

A member of the agave family, Mexico

Sedum plants in Olympic National Park, Washington

Detail of cactus spines

Rows of cactus spines

"Forest" of prickly pear, Baja California
Following page: *Ice crystals*

INDEX OF PHOTOGRAPHY

All photographs courtesy of The Image Bank, except where indicated *